7 QUESTIONS WISE WOMEN ASK

Kingsley Okonkwo

7 QUESTIONS WISE WOMEN ASK

Copyright © 2021, 2020, 2010
Kingsley Okonkwo

ISBN 9798851130533

All rights reserved under International Copyright Law. Contents and/or cover may not be reproduced in any form without the express written consent of the publisher.

Unless otherwise indicated, all Scripture quotations are taken from the King James Version of the Bible.

To contact the author

Tel: 08077714411, 08077714413.

Contents

◇◇◇◇◇◇◇◇◇◇◇◇◇◇◇◇◇

PREFACE 5

INTRODUCTION 11

QUESTION 1 17
Why Me?

QUESTION 2 27
Do I Know Him Well Enough?

QUESTION 3 35
Who Are His Influences?

QUESTION 4 43
Are We Compatible?

QUESTION 5 49
Is He Responsible?

QUESTION 6 65
When?

QUESTION 7 73
Is He Born-Again?

FINAL WORD 81

SURRENDER TO CHRIST 83

PREFACE

Women are largely emotional beings. Most women thrive on the health of their relationships with others which is why a good percentage of the challenges a woman would face in her life will be connected to her relationships. The relationships in a woman's life matter to her, but the most important of these relationships is the one she has with men.

I have seen great potentials destroyed and destinies aborted simply because a woman made an unenlightened or uninformed choice concerning the man she would spend her life with. In my work as a relationship coach and marriage counsellor for over two decades, I have observed a particular pattern with women and their relationships with men. Many women tend to repeat the same mistakes in their relationship with men regardless of who the man is. I can't count the number of women who come to me in tears because a man treated them poorly and they are frustrated by the fact that they don't know how to end the cycle of heartbreaks and disappointments in their relationships.

The prevailing culture in our society today is such that women are under undue pressure to get married, especially when they fall within a certain age bracket. This pressure intensifies when everyone around her seems to be getting married and having children. For instance, she receives an invitation to the wedding of one of her childhood friends who happens to be a few years younger than her, her third cousin just had another baby, she has to attend the baby shower of one of her

• *Preface* •

colleagues, her friendly neighbour invites her to her child's one-year birthday party, and even her younger sibling is having an engagement party soon. Everywhere she turns, someone is getting married and she feels excluded and very conscious of the fact that she is still single. To make matters worse, she can't fast track the process of changing her marital status. She is expected to wait patiently for a man to like her enough to ask for her hand in marriage. Society does not allow her to walk up to a man she likes and propose to him but they expect her to get married on time. As time goes on, her desperation builds and the moment a man proposes to her she is in a hurry to get the ring on her finger as fast as possible. She is willing to settle for a life with this man even when she knows deep down in her heart that he is not the right man for her. For a woman at this stage, the goal is to get married and not to marry right.

If you are going through a situation that is similar to the scenario I just painted, I understand your pain. But I want you to know that you deserve the best no matter the odds. You don't have to settle for less. Think about it, if you have waited for this long even though you did not know that you had this level of patience in you, you might as well get it right. There's no point in waiting to be married only to end up marrying the wrong person.

Can I tell you a secret? Marriage is difficult when you enter into it for the wrong reasons. And some of those wrong reasons include getting married because of family pressure, yielding to societal pressure or giving in to your fear of getting old and dying alone as a single woman. There are basic factors that are crucial to the survival of a marriage. These are the things one must consider before getting married. But, a desperate woman would naturally overlook or ignore them to her own disadvantage. Marriage is not the kind of institution you can drop out of, at the slightest inconvenience, to start all over again with someone else. Before you agree to marry anyone you must study his character, ask the right questions and be patient enough to get the right answers. You will be saving yourself a lot of heartache by doing this because the decision of who to marry is not based on a person's looks, financial status or level of exposure.

Introduction

Relationships are not for fun like society has painted it to be. It is a period of time where you get to know the person you are about to commit the rest of your life to, in order to find out if he is fit for the marathon called marriage. When a company is about to hire new staff, they mean business. Even when the human resource person is being friendly, he or she knows the exact qualities to look out for in the person who would fill the vacant position in their company. So when the person lightens up the mood with jokes so you can relax, the aim is to create an atmosphere where you can be yourself and be assessed properly.

Marriage is serious business. Beyond how you feel about each other, there are basic things that must be in place for your marriage to stand the test of time. And those things are determined at the foundation stage, long before you say "I do". When you date a man for the mere fun of it, you will have your fun but only one person will leave that relationship smiling and that person will most likely not be you. And that's because women are generally more emotional beings; they thrive on relationships. Many single women just can't imagine themselves being alone at any point in their adult life. So you find them holding on to relationships that are clearly not working for them, which won't be the case if they had set the right goal or destination for the relationship in the first place.

Having a clear purpose for any

• *Introduction* •

relationship will go a long way in helping you make good decisions in the course of your relationship. And the right goal is to be ***happily married.*** Anyone can get married but it takes more to enjoy a happy marriage. It is better to be single and happy than to be married and sad. It is easy to get carried away with the excitement of a romantic relationship, especially a new one, that you lose sight of the goal. For instance, if you drive a particular car for a few years you will notice that once you accelerate towards the speed limit, the car will start to jerk as a sign that you are pushing it towards the speed limit. A new car, however, will indulge you to whatever speed level you want to drive on even when it's dangerous to your life and other road users. Most people drive their relationships like new cars. They are on the speed lane enjoying the ride with little thought to their safety or destination.

• 7 Questions Wise Women Ask •

The questions in this book are like your speedometer. They are designed to help you measure your progress in a relationship and know whether you are driving safely on the right road or you are cruising on a highway to destruction.

Marriage is a long trip. It is not an end in itself but it's a means to an end, and that end is fulfilment. A person who is not fulfilled in her marriage will be discontented for a very long time, and a discontented person is vulnerable to all kinds of temptations. So, it is important that you make adequate preparations and ask the right questions before you hand over the rest of your life to that man you are considering. You have to ensure that he is worth it.

The questions you are about to encounter in this book are not questions like "Do you love him? Does he love you? Do you

• *Introduction* •

love him more or less than he loves you?" No, those are vague questions and their answers will not serve as a good yardstick to measure if you are in the right place in your relationship or even with the right person. It is true that many people don't know what love truly is. Most times when people ask if you are in love with someone, what they want to know is if you have butterflies in your stomach for him. The reality is that love is way beyond "catching feelings" for someone.

In asking these questions, your approach is crucial. You don't have to grab a seat, call the man who is seeking your hand in marriage and start interrogating him. No. Some of the questions I listed in this book are things you might need to ask yourself, some will require that you ask him subtly or indirectly and others are things you just need to observe and take note of as the relationship or friendship progresses.

But, you must be smart about it. The strategy is not to make it so obvious that you are looking for the answers or else, any sharp guy will play smart and give you "perfect" answers that he knows you want to hear, even though they are all lies.

Now, let's get right into the seven questions wise women ask. It's my prayer that these questions will guide you in making the right decision and ultimately help you build a blissful marriage.

1

WHY ME?

If I were a woman, the first thing I would want to know is why someone wants to marry me. Think about it: out of all the women he could have asked to be his wife, why did he choose you? Aren't you curious to know? You will be amazed at the reasons he may have for wanting to marry you. As a marriage counsellor, I've heard the most amazing responses from men when I asked questions like, "Why do you want to get married?" One said, "I'm getting old. I need to settle down." This fellow is after the benefits of being married, whoever he gets married to doesn't matter to him. Another man said, "I'm the only son of my parents and they are pressuring me to give them a grandchild." That man was looking for a baby-making factory. He may not bother himself with loving his wife as long as she can give him babies. There are many more odd reasons like these two but I'm sure you already get where I am going with this. When a man proposes to you, ask him, "Why me?" If you don't know why he asked you to marry him, you won't know what to improve on when the need arises. If he married you because of the shape of your body, then get ready to buy gym equipment for you to maintain your figure or your marriage may not last. Of course, it is not good to marry a woman just because of her body structure; however, WHY a man decides to marry you is pivotal and will greatly impact your marriage. And when you ask him why he wants to marry you, don't let him tell you sweet nothings like "I like your lips, your hips, and your fingertips."

• *Why Me?* •

It may sound romantic and rhyme well but there is really no meaning to it. Sweet nothings are usually as the name implies, sweet nothings. I'll share a few stories to buttress this point:

A couple was having problems in their marriage because, according to the man, the wife couldn't keep the house tidy to his standard. After reporting his wife to their pastor, the pastor asked him why he chose to marry his wife in the first place and the young man said, "I married her because she was fun to be with, pleasant and very understanding." Based on his response the pastor asked him further, "Is she no longer fun to be with? Has she become unpleasant over time? Has she stopped being understanding?" His response to all these questions was "No." So the Pastor told him, "You see, nothing has changed. Your wife is still as good as she was when you married her. Hire someone else to do the cleaning." Once this man was reminded of his reason for marrying his wife, his frustrations with her vanished. Your reason for marrying your spouse is one of the things that will keep your marriage going.

An excited young man once told me that his reason for seeking a certain woman's hand in marriage was her extraordinary skills at pounding yam. *Pounded yam is a choice meal in this part of the world.* But can you imagine someone wanting to marry you just because of your outstanding cooking skills?

A young preacher noticed a certain lady's unusual interest in his well-being. He talked to her about it and got to know that the lady was interested in being his wife. So he asked her why she wanted to marry him and she replied, "I love the kind of

• *Why Me?* •

ministry you are involved in." Now, this young preacher had a youth ministry at the time. While it may be true that the lady has a passion for youth ministry, she wasn't going to marry the youth ministry. She was going to marry the man and men are usually very different from the ministry they have been called to in the same way that what a man does for a living can be different from who he is at home.

A preacher preaches under a divine influence known as the anointing which is the Spirit of God helping him carry out his function in his office as a preacher. The same man who preaches up a storm and heals the sick with a mighty demonstration of God's power could snore loudly at night or stain his clothes during meals and he may not know how to chew his food with his mouth closed. You can't expect him to preach at home because he preaches in the church. You must separate the man from his gift. This reminds me of a story I once heard:

A certain woman came to church while the service was on with her two children and luggage. She went straight to the altar where the pastor stood preaching and sat there. The congregation murmured amongst themselves because they didn't understand what was going on. This woman knew that the murmur in the congregation was about her but she ignored it and made herself comfortable beside the pastor who happened to be her husband. When asked what the problem was, she told the church members that she wants to marry the pastor. By this time, the people were genuinely concerned about her mental state because to the best of their knowledge she was already the pastor's wife. Explaining further, she said,

"The person you all know as your pastor and my husband are two different men. This one on the altar is a kind and patient man but the one at home, that I live with, is a wicked man." She was trying to let them know that once the man is done discharging his duties as the pastor of the church, another version of him who is a bad husband and father comes home to live with them and she was tired of it. It is a funny story that gets you thinking every time you hear it but it is the sad reality of some women in their marital homes.

I used preachers as examples for you to know how serious this issue is. When you fall in love with a man's gift or abilities and not his person or his character, you are setting yourself up for trouble. You must learn to separate the man from his ministry or vocation because you will always have the man but what he does might change.

If a man's reason for wanting to make you his wife is not based on character traits like meekness, intelligence or your sense of purpose then you are already setting yourself up for a broken marriage. It must be about who you are; your qualities or virtues, and not your gifts, talents, or beauty.

A young lady told me that her relationship had ended, so I asked her how she got to know the man she had a relationship with and what led to the breakup. From what she said, they both sang in the choir and their voices harmonized well. After hearing her out, I told her that it's possible that the young man realized that he had better harmony with another lady in the choir apart from her. Is it not amazing that anyone would start something as important as a relationship based on how well her voice sounds with someone else's?

Why Me?

For me, I married my wife because she is godly, intelligent and understanding and today, she is even more intelligent and understanding. The qualities I saw when I married her are still present and we are still very happy.

2

Do I Know Him Well Enough?

I am not referring to how long you have known him but rather to how well you know him. These are two very different things. It is possible to know someone for a long time and still not know who they really are as it is possible to meet someone and feel like you have known them all your life. Some women are married to total strangers because when they met their husband they felt a connection with him; they had chemistry. So they went on romantic dates and never talked about things that would matter in their future, just like when you hang out with your friends and talk about everything and everyone for hours.

You completely enjoy the company, conversation and food but when you really think about it, all you did was gist at the end of the day.

Relationships that last are not rushed to the next level, especially if you consider that you have the rest of your life to spend with this person. As they say, speed kills. So before you commit your life to a man, invest time to consciously get to know who he really is.

Cultivate genuine friendship with him. It is best to let the relationship grow out of friendship because when the excitement of the wedding wears off and the children come, friendship with your spouse is what your marriage will thrive on. So let the friendship grow. Let it blossom. Know him well enough before you begin to think of walking down the aisle with him.

Do I Know Him Well Enough?

Everyone puts on his or her best behaviour on a first date. This is because the goal is to get married. You will catch yourself saying that you are fine when he asks you how you are doing when in fact you are not fine. And when the menu comes, you might just request for portable water or something light even when you are very hungry. It's all an act. But in a friendship, you will get comfortable with each other enough to be yourself and that's the point.

Unfortunately, many people breeze past the friendship part to get to the romance not knowing that they just missed the most important part of the relationship. Take a moment to think about the people in your life. You will discover that the people you can honestly say that you know are the ones with whom you can be yourself with. They are your close friends with no strings attached. Romance has a way of clouding your sense of judgment.

Genuinely desire true friendships in your life because it is the soil where true love blossoms. People are more disposed to let their guards down with you as a friend than when there is something else involved in their relationship with you.

Don't allow the fact that you are getting old put you in a desperate mode such that you walk around with an *I-must-get-married* attitude. A desperate woman is easy to spot in a crowd. She is prone to making bad choices and settling for the wrong kinds of men. I am yet to see anyone make good decisions under pressure. In most cases, the person ends up shortchanging herself.

I met a young man who narrated his experience in the search of a life partner. He met a beautiful young woman who readily agreed with everything he said. He thought it was a bit strange so he

• *Do I Know Him Well Enough?* •

intentionally said some conflicting things just to know how the lady would respond. He would tell her that he disliked someone because he was indecisive and she would agree with him that the person cannot be trusted. Then speaking about the same person, he would say, "Well, the guy is not so bad. I think he is okay." And the lady would also agree without asking him very obvious questions as to why he was contradicting himself. She so desperately wanted to impress him that she was acting like she doesn't have a mind of her own. Her goal was to impress him by all means and he found it repulsive.

Please, be yourself. Don't buy a club's jersey because the man you like belongs to that particular club. You don't have to be a football fan because he is one. Remember, the goal is not to impress him. Don't pretend to be someone you are not just to get to the altar because you will have to continue acting that drama for the rest of your life. Any attempt to stop the act would invite problems into your marriage. Don't start what you cannot finish. Pretence may get you to the altar but it won't help you in marriage. Eventually, you will get tired of acting and your true nature will reveal itself. When he eventually finds out you don't like football, and a host of other things you pretended to like just because you wanted to marry him, I can assure you that the consequences will not be good. Nobody likes to know that they've been deceived for so long, especially by someone they love or trust. So drop the pretence now, it will do you no good.

One of the qualities that attracted me to my wife is her ability to be herself. We went to the same secondary school but I

• *Do I Know Him Well Enough?* •

didn't quite know her. I had my first real encounter with her ten years after we graduated from college. A couple of my classmates and I had gone to her house to continue discussions on the reunion we were planning and she came out to talk to us. Note, it was already dark by that time of day so I could not see her face clearly. But, I could hear her voice and from the few statements she made that day, I could tell that she was smart and intelligent. I liked what I heard so I decided to investigate further and today, we are married. She wasn't trying to pretend or impress me. She was just herself and that drew me to her.

When you pretend to be who you are not, you might miss the right person for you. Let's assume that someone has been praying for someone like you; someone down-to-earth and self-confident. Then he walks into a restaurant hoping to see a girl that can eat *eba* (an african delicacy) with her bare hands and you know you like to eat *eba* with your hand but because you feel there are important people in the room, you go for a fork and knife although you don't know how to use it. So while you are struggling with the meat, he enters and doesn't even notice you because you are just like everybody else.

The truth is, there is someone for everyone. You have to be yourself for the right person for you to find you.

3

WHO ARE HIS INFLUENCES?

A man's influences are the people he knows and has given access into his life to either speak to him or just be a part of his life. The majority of a man's influences are his friends and people hardly outgrow their circle of friends. You must have heard the popular sayings like *"Show me your friend and I will tell you who you are"* or *"birds of a feather, flock together."* A person is largely a reflection of who his closest friends are.

> *"He that walks with the wise shall be wise but a companion of fools shall be destroyed."*
>
> —PROVERBS 13:20 [KJV]

When an unwise person starts to keep company with wise people, over time he will come to learn wisdom. Such is the power of influence.

The reverse can also be the case. So ask yourself, do his friends drink? If they do, he will soon start drinking. And even if he manages not to drink, there is a chance that he might get hurt due to drunk driving from one of his friends. There have been cases where a drunk driver in the company of his friends had an accident while driving and killed everyone in the car including himself.

Who are his *role models*? If the person he looks up to is a man of one wife and a few side chicks, then get ready to deal with such things. Who are his *mentors*? Your mentor is the prophecy of your future. If his mentor has been divorced a few times, there's a possibility that he would do the same.

• *Who Are His Influences?* •

Who does he listen to? If he listens to the wrong people and takes their advice, he would believe the wrong things and behave the wrong way. You must know these things about him because having a bad mentor, role model or bad friends is worse than having none at all.

Some men are *lone rangers* or what is popularly called a *one-man army*. A lone ranger believes he knows it all so he needs no one's advice. If he is a believer, he will say things like "Jesus is my mentor." The average guy will say, "Nobody was there for me when I was struggling my way through life." Men with such mindsets will have a problem submitting to spiritual authorities so beware of him.

Do not marry a freelance Christian. A freelance Christian is someone who believes that church is in the heart and so has a habit of moving from one church to another under the guise that he is looking for a good church where he can finally settle down. A church or local assembly is a depot of God's blessings. When a man is unable to commit to a church family, even angels will have a hard time guessing where he will be on Sunday mornings. The man you should marry must belong to a church where he is known and where he serves. He must have a pastor he submits to. Without such structures in his life, he is a failure going somewhere to happen.

Do not marry a man who is not accountable to spiritual authority because he will not consult anyone when he wants to deal with you. And you can't report him to anyone. Marry a man who has someone that can hold him accountable for his words and actions. I remember when my wife and I went to see one of my mentors and right in the middle of our conversation he asked my wife how married life has been. She responded, "It's very fine, Sir. Don't worry if he misbehaves, I have your number. You will be the first person I would reach out to." We all laughed over it but that is how it should be. If I am misbehaving, she has someone she can ask to intervene. Many great men have been destroyed because they had no mentors. There was no one to caution them while they were making the wrong decisions.

Every man needs to have someone he respects who can step in with wise counsel when he needs it. Someone who can keep him accountable. Someone his wife can ask to intervene when she feels like she cannot reach or communicate her concerns to him effectively. Examples of situations where a mentor or spiritual authority will come in handy includes if he wants to make a decision that can hurt his family like using the house as collateral for a business he doesn't know anything about, or if he starts to receive strange calls and texts from strange women, or if he starts attending strange meetings and has to sleep overnight every day of the week in some hotel or if he travels and nobody knows about it in his office yet he says he is on an official assignment. You need to have someone he respects that you can call on speed dial. Everybody needs accountability.

When we went on air with *Love, Dating and Marriage* on TV, I sought counsel from people who had been on Television long before me. They gave me insightful information that helped me a great deal. They told me things that are helpful to my ministry even till today. Many great people have been destroyed because they

· *Who Are His Influences?* ·

had no mentors. I believe that John the Baptist lost his life prematurely partly because he meddled with someone else's personal life (See Luke 3:19-20). He left his baptism ministry and gave unsolicited advice to a political figure. I believe that if he had a mentor, he could have been saved from premature death. Mentors are there to protect us from torment. Your mentor is not necessarily your friend so don't expect him to tell you what you want to hear. His job is to tell you the truth and that is what you need.

4

ARE WE COMPATIBLE?

One of the ways you can ensure that you are happily married is to ensure that you and your life partner are compatible.

Can two people walk together without agreeing on the direction?
—AMOS 3:3 [NLT]

Compatibility is your ability to live together, work well, be like-minded and well matched in most areas of life with someone. Anything apart from this suggests that you are divided; you believe different things and are pursuing different agendas, which defeats the very purpose of the marriage. You need

• 7 Questions Wise Women Ask •

to have singleness of purpose with the person you intend to marry. This is very important.

> *And the Lord God said, it is not good that man should be alone. I will make him a helpmeet.*
> —GENESIS 2:18 [KJV]

The word *helpmeet* is actually two words in one. And it means *help* (an assistant) that is *meet* (suitable and adaptable). You were not made to be suitable and adaptable to everyone.

Some women shut the doors on their destinies the day they said, "I do" to a man they were not suitable for or adaptable to. If you don't want to be a housewife, do not marry a man who wants a housewife because you are not suitable for each other. But a woman whose dream is to be a housewife will be thrilled to have such a man as a husband. A woman who finds fulfilment in climbing the ladder in her career would be unwise to marry a man who won't let her work outside the home. They will both frustrate each other. When a woman complains that she has lost her passion for life because her husband would not let her be herself, I am quick to gently remind her that she saw the warning signs but chose to ignore them because she was under pressure to get married.

Here are a few questions that will help you know if you are compatible with your partner.

- What does he think about a husband-and-wife relationship?
- Does he think the man is the lord of lords and the king of kings who can make decisions without consulting his wife?

- Does he believe his word is law and not to be questioned even when he is advised otherwise?
- Do you believe and think alike spiritually?
- Are you going in the same direction?
- Do you have the same family values?
- Are your life visions related?

You must ask these questions and know the answers before you take that relationship further. There are several Christian denominations that do not agree with each other on doctrinal matters. For instance, I have preached in churches where men wear earrings and I have also preached in churches where women don't wear any kind of jewelry. A man and a woman from each of these churches will have a hard time in marriage because they don't even believe alike spiritually.

• *Are We Compatible?* •

Just because you are both born again, speak the same language and/or even attend the same church does not mean you can live with each other. You must consider other basic compatibility issues like social interaction, physical attraction, intellect, and purpose. These things are important as not every Christian is great at social interactions, not all can stimulate you mentally or engage you in intelligent conversations and you may never be physically attracted to everyone. Remember, you don't have to manage anyone.

Marriage is not about who started the race first, it's about who finishes well. It is like a marathon. You need to prepare well so that you don't faint along the way or even pull out of the race totally. Prepare well. Ask the right questions. Take heed to these little things.

5

Is He Responsible?

This question is a very serious one for me because it seems like there are more irresponsible men on earth today than there are responsible men. Keep this in mind; the mere fact that someone has the physical anatomy of a man does not make him a man. There is more to being a man than just being male. Families can only be run by men and not boys. That is how God ordained it. And the one thing that separates boys from men is *responsibility*.

Responsibility in marriage is defined by three things and any man who cannot do any of these is a boy and has no business proposing to you. Even if he does, it is in your interest as a wise woman to refuse his proposal until he can get his acts together. The three things are as follows:

CAN HE PRESIDE?

A man must be able to make sound decisions and give the right direction to the family. That's the basics of leadership. Some married women are shocked to realize the man they are married to is incapable of guiding the affairs of their home confidently with authority. Don't get carried away with the excitement of love and romance that you commit your life to a man with no dreams, vision, plans or even character. If you discover that his dream is to enjoy life, look good and keep his reputation in the public eye while you serve his every need, do not get involved with him. You know a leader by what he is already doing with his life.

· *Is He Responsible?* ·

You will find him committed to being a better person, planning for his future and making financial investments. Don't be deceived by how much he is earning at the moment and his promise of a very colourful tomorrow. All that must be backed by solid patterns that show that at each point in his life he was busy doing something meaningful and productive. If he is unable to make sound decisions about his own financial life, it is very unlikely that he will do any better with you in the picture. Let's assume that his income is a hundred and twenty thousand naira now, in a short while that amount will not be able to sustain him because he will have a family to take care of. So, before he marries you, he must have a plan to consistently improve his financial life, if not he is on the path to poverty and if you marry him, so are you.

Do not commit yourself to a man that will jeopardize not only your own future but the future of your children as well. Marry a man who can make sound decisions no matter what the circumstances are.

Avoid mummy's boys. A mummy's boy is a man who will do nothing without his mom's approval. He would ask for her opinion even to the kind of house he should live in with his wife. It is in this part of the world that you see a full-grown man living with his father. He will get married in his father's house and raise his child in that same house. When the child grows, just like his father, he will also marry in that house and have his children there as well. Which clearly goes against what the Bible instructs us to do.

> *Therefore shall a man leave his father and mother and shall cleave to his wife and they shall be one flesh.*
> —GENESIS 2:24 [KJV]

Is He Responsible?

There's nothing wrong with a man honouring his parents by listening to them and taking good advice from them on some issues. However, he must understand that the final decision is his as the head of his own home. He doesn't have the luxury to run to his father or mother every time an issue arises in his marriage. It is up to him to know what is good for his family and to ensure that it gets done.

CAN HE PROVIDE?

Do not marry a jobless man. Gone are the days when a man would use "No one is giving me a job" or "Life is hard" as excuses for idleness. Life is not easy for even the richest man because he has to work hard to manage and maintain his wealth. If a man doesn't have a job, he can employ himself by creating a job for himself. A business person once said to me, "There is no easy way to be a man. Once you successfully tackle a problem, another one arises." And he's right. Being a man involves tackling issues as they keep arising until you leave this earth.

When God made man, He said to him, "Be fruitful and multiply." Every man has a God-given ability to be successful and overcome any limitation in life. Nothing can stop a man who knows this truth from being successful. All he has to do is to apply himself to something and there are several options he can explore. He can either start a business or learn a trade or even render menial services and be paid for it. Nigeria is a place with many opportunities and the rich among us can testify to this. It is unacceptable and ungodly for a man not to have something he is doing.

• *Is He Responsible?* •

> *For even when we were with you, we gave you this rule: If a man will not work, let him not eat.*
> —2 THESSALONIANS 3:10 [NLT]

A lazy man is not qualified to eat. And if he can't feed himself, a wife is too much for him to handle. The aim of the instruction in the Scripture above is to use hunger as a motivating factor to get the lazy man off his feet and on his way to find something to do. Every man is designed to earn a living. It is sad to see women set very low standards for the men in their lives by supporting their irresponsibility. Like a toddler who falls a few times while learning how to walk, a man must build his financial muscles by putting his hands to work at something until he gets positive results. When he experiences failure, he should learn from it and keep moving. Failure is not an excuse for him to sit on his hands and do nothing. There is no lion in the streets. *(See Proverbs 26:13)* Don't pity a broke and jobless man and give him food. It won't do him any good. Hunger is the only recommended antidote for a lazy man. It was hunger that drove the Prodigal son out of his wayward lifestyle back to his father's house to work. *(See Luke 15: 11-20)*. Don't marry a man who takes you out to lunch or buys gifts for you with pocket money he collects from his parents. That's a child right there. A man must be able to provide.

Before God gave Adam a wife, he ensured that he had something he was doing *(See Genesis 2:15)*. Part of Eve's assignment was to help Adam get his work done. *(See Genesis 2:18)* If Adam had no job, what would he need a helpmeet for? A man is better off with a low paying job than he is with none at all. Work is a confidence booster for men.

Is He Responsible?

A lazy man will abandon you and your kids in the future when he realizes that he cannot provide for you. We have heard stories of women who were abandoned in the hospitals by their husbands when they gave birth to twins or triplets. The husband ran away because he knew he couldn't afford the hospital bills. Many married women today are overburdened with the responsibility of catering for their families all by themselves. Some of them saw the signs of irresponsibility in the man before they got married considering his record of accomplishment, but they hoped that the man would change. Whenever I hear a woman say, "He will change," it is evident that she knows very little about how men work. Men get tougher and more set in their ways as they grow older. It is wise to be mindful of the man's character today because any necessary change he has not adopted before he met you might be difficult for him to embrace in the future.

CAN HE PROTECT?

One of the principal assignments God has given to the man is to protect his home. This quality is at the core of what defines responsibility in a marriage. Are you convinced that the man you are about to marry can protect your family from danger or will he rather hide behind you and nudge you forward? Will he be able to protect you from your in-laws if he has to or will he always be tongue-tied and helpless before his mother?

When I hear women complain bitterly about their quarrelsome mothers-in-law, I am quick to ask them where their husbands were when all that was happening. It would take a boy and not a

• *Is He Responsible?* •

man to allow his own wife to be terrorized by anyone anywhere, not to mention in her own home. He must be able to protect you even from his mother. Can you imagine a man saying, "My mother does not like my wife. She maltreats her and I don't know what to do about it." A man should not allow things to get out of hand to this extent under his watch. My mother has never insulted my wife. She wouldn't do that because my wife is my wife and no one else's. My mother may not like what my wife does sometimes but as long as I like it, that's all that matters. It is my responsibility to let my wife know if there is anything she does that I don't like. I don't need anybody to do that on my behalf.

This is why you must not marry a mummy's boy. I want to believe that you don't want a husband who will go to his mother's house to look for what to eat when he has you at home or who would look for any excuse he can come up with just to be with his mom because he is used to the way she pampers him. Confirm that the man you are about to marry is able and willing to protect you from anyone you need protection from before you commit to him.

It's natural for mothers to treat their children as babies even when they are adults. That is just how a mother's love works. It always cares affectionately no matter how old and grey-haired the child gets. It is up to the child in question to know where to draw the line and respectfully let his mother know that he is an adult. On this note, I pray that fathers would be more proactive in helping their wives bring a balance to their relationship with their children, especially their sons.

• *Is He Responsible?* •

On a side note, a man who already beats you while he is dating you is the one you need to be protected from. Stop making costly excuses for his bad character like, "But I am the one who provoked him." Stop that! No matter the level of provocation, a man should never beat a woman. Only weak men resort to physical violence as a way of bringing a woman under control. You will not find such men beating up their fellow men in the streets. If he has that amount of free energy in him and does not know what to do with it, he can enroll for professional boxing and make good money for himself rather than use it to bruise and batter you for free at home. But he wouldn't do that because he is a coward who will not even dare to fight men his size and age. No, he will not. If there is a confrontation with another man, he will rather make peace than fight.

• 7 Questions Wise Women Ask •

As a Pastor, I have heard all sorts of disturbing excuses from women why the men in their lives beat them up. Some say their husbands beat them up to discipline them. It is not in any man's place to discipline you whether he is your husband, fiancé, boyfriend or brother. He can correct you with his words in love but certainly not with his fists or belt. Any man who physically abuses you will not be able to protect you from anyone because he is the one you need to be protected from.

The man who says, "If you love me, you will sleep with me" is not interested in taking the relationship any further than just having sex with you. A man who has your best interest at heart will never say such a thing to you. You are worth more than rubies so don't sell yourself short by indulging such men. Having sex with

Is He Responsible?

someone other than your husband is a sin before God. If a man wants you that much, let him do the needful and marry you. Any man who cannot preside over you, protect you and provide for you is the exact kind of man you should stay away from.

6

WHEN?

Imagine that on a Saturday evening, while watching movies at home with some of your female friends who came over to visit, a friend knocks on your door with a bouquet of flowers and a gift bag in his hand. You are surprised to see him at the door because you were not expecting him and it's not your birthday. He hands you the bouquet of flowers as he enters and says 'Hi' to your friends. While everyone shifts their gaze back to the movie, suddenly he is standing right in front of you and then goes down on one knee holding out a small velvet box. As he opens it, you see a gold-plated engagement ring. By now, your friends have paused the movie and have brought out their phones to record the live movie happening in front of them. The young man, encouraged by this begins to make his speech of how amazing you are and how you mean the world to him and when he is done, *which is usually when his knee really starts to hurt,* he pops the big question, "Will you marry me?" At this point, everyone holds their breath in hope that you will say **"Yes"** And when you do, they erupt with shouts of joy and congratulations.

Ladies usually get carried away at this stage that they forget to ask the very important question, **"When?"** You need to know the answer to this question before you accept any proposal from any man. It is important that you know if his plans align with yours. If for instance, you are about thirty years old and a man makes a proposal to you with the intention of

• *When?* •

getting married to you in the next five years, wouldn't you want to be informed ahead? I have seen people old enough to get married who courted for almost a decade and never got married. Prolonged courtship usually does not end up in marriage. It is risky to wait for a man for too long.

> *When there is no vision, the people perish but he that keepeth the law, happy is he."*
> — PROVERBS 29:18 [KJV]

To perish in simpler English means to cast off restraint, to grow idle, to enter an inferior condition or to run wild or to go crazy. The law of life states that there must be a vision for everything we do. Without a vision, nothing works. For most things in life, you need something to look forward to for hope and encouragement when the going gets tough. Imagine that after many years of trying, you finally gained admission into the university and with great excitement, you go to the school administrative building to find out more about the course you have been given. "Please how long will this course take?" You ask. Only to hear, "Erm, we can't really say. The duration of the course largely depends on the student. Some of the last set of students that gained admission to our campus for this course have been here for over ten years. They hope to graduate someday. So, you just go ahead and start whenever you want to and when you graduate is when you graduate." Now, would you go ahead to enroll in a school like this? I hope not. In the same manner, do not play games with your life. Do not date or court anyone indefinitely.

If he really wants to marry you, he should

· *When?* ·

tell you when he plans to do that so you can know if you have the time to wait for him or not. In this part of the world, a man can be all over you for two whole years and then wake up one day to tell you, "My dear, I've been troubled in my spirit for a while now and I've been praying about it. I perceive that the Holy Spirit is speaking to me concerning some crucial aspects of my life and destiny. So far, what He has been telling me is hard to do but who am I to disobey the Holy Spirit. The call of God upon my life requires that I..." The point is that he can't continue the relationship with you. And just like that, you would have wasted two good years of your life, energy, and opportunity to build a lasting relationship with the right person. As a woman, it is to your disadvantage in every way to date someone without a specific timeline.

One of my daughters in the Lord shared with us how her ex called her, while she was on her way to pick their wedding cards from the printer and told her not to go because he needed to see her urgently. So, she hurried to get to where he was. When she got there, he told her, "Babe, I need some time." At first, she didn't understand what he meant. What could he possibly need time for halfway into their wedding preparations? So, she calmly asked him, "how much time do you need?" And he gave the classic response that has zero commitment written all over it, "'I'm not sure how long. But please, just give me some time before we can go on with this wedding."

What do you think? Should she wait for him? For how long? As exciting as a marriage proposal is, please insist on knowing when?

When?

The fact that a man wants to marry you is great. But you must ensure that he has a concrete plan for when he wants to marry you. Anyone who is serious about planning any kind of event will definitely have a date in mind.

Like I said earlier, the woman is most affected when a relationship lasts for too long and ends abruptly for no good reason. She would need enough time and care to heal from the hurt and overcome the psychological effect of having to see every other man through the eyes of the person who disappointed her. It is not in her nature to dust it off as though nothing happened and try again with someone else. And even if she can, what are the chances that she will find another man so soon. A man, on the other hand, can marry someone else the day after he breaks up with a woman. He can see someone else the next day and marry her. He can go to the village to line up all the women there and choose one or he can go to the market or mall and pick one woman from there and that is all. Many women have been kept waiting and today, they cannot move forward. Do not waste your life.

7

IS HE BORN-AGAIN?

We live in a world where being born again is seen as something that has no bearing on marriage. Some are quick to defend their stand by saying that our parents of old were not born again yet their marriages lasted longer than most of the marriages we see today. But as a marriage counsellor who enjoys a quarrel-free marriage, I can assure you that what our parents had cannot be compared to a marriage that is built on the principles of God.

One of the purposes of marriage, according to God's Word, is to raise a godly offspring. The unsaved man, or someone who has not accepted Christ as his Lord and Saviour, cannot fulfil this purpose of marriage because he needs the God-factor in him to produce a godly seed. The process of raising a godly seed includes how a child is born and nurtured.

Being born again is much more than going to church regularly. There are many church goers who are not saved. It is about letting Christ come into your heart to change your nature, principally. I have been a sinner and now I am saved so I know the difference. The difference is so much. They are worlds apart.

When I was in the world, I was not an amateur sinner. Just name anything that is called sin and you can bet that I have tried it before. My slogan then used to be, "If you can conceive it, I can do it." I did all sorts of bad things and I can assure you that there is no profit in it. There is a prince of the power of the air operating in the world.

• Is He Born-Again? •

And you hath he quickened, who were dead in trespasses and sins; Wherein in time past ye walked according to the course of this world, according to the prince of the power of the air, the spirit that now worketh in the children of disobedience: Among whom also we all had our conversation in times past in the lusts of our flesh, fulfilling the desires of the flesh and of the mind; and were by nature the children of wrath, even as others.

— EPHESIANS 2:1-3 [KJV]

This implies that everybody is influenced by a spirit whether positive or negative. It is either you are filled with the Holy Spirit or with an evil spirit. It is natural for humans to do negative things: to lie, steal and kill. But when Christ changed our nature through our faith in His sacrifice on the cross, it became natural for us to speak the truth, give and make alive. In Christ, we have the right through our right standing with God to bear the fruit of the Spirit which is a life that is like that of Christ.

Being born again involves acknowledging our sinful state, accepting the payment that Christ made for our sins on the cross, receiving the free gift of eternal life and grace to live right that Jesus made available to us and then willingly surrendering our lives completely to Christ. It also means dying to sin and coming alive to God and His ways because you are now born of the Word of God and the Spirit of God. One of the benefits of being born again is that the nature of God is activated in you. The laws of God get written in your heart such that you can be led by the Spirit of God into the will of God. You start to desire the things of God and love to do what pleases Him. Living right becomes appealing to you and something you enjoy. It ceases to be a struggle because as you fellowship with God, you will begin to see sin for what it really is — destruction and death.

Marriage is God's idea. The spiritual dimension of any marriage is crucial to its success as much as, if not more than, the physical dimension. But many would rather focus on the physical aspects of a marriage than the spiritual aspects. So, who you decide to marry matters a lot. It matters the kind of spirit controlling the person you have decided to spend the rest of your life with. We honour God when we obey His principles for marriage. And He blesses us with the benefits of obedience which is a happy and fulfilling marriage.

When you consider the way some Christians behave these days, it is clear that they have forgotten what it means to be born again. Being born again is not old fashioned, as many would like to think, Jesus gave His life for that very purpose.

He could have just given us motivational speeches and gone back to heaven but our salvation required that He laid down His very life. He died to rid us of our fallen nature and give us access to the very life and nature of God. He died so that by faith in Him we can become the children of God.

It is important you note that the human capacity for evil is incredibly high. The unsaved man is selfish and wicked *(See Jeremiah 17:9)*. Someone said, "Anything that is human is not alien to me." What that means is that if any human being has ever done anything, good or bad, then I also have the capacity to do the same thing because I am human. Without the Spirit of God actively working in us and leading us in the right path, there is no limit to the extent we can go to do evil. A quick look at the News channels and horrors all around us proves this.

Is He Born-Again?

A godly marriage is impossible without the love of Christ. The very nature of this love implies that a person who is not born again does not have it in him to give. The love of God is poured into our hearts by the Holy Spirit. *(See Romans 5:5b)* It is with that love that we can love others efficiently and effectively. One of the most outstanding qualities of this love is that it is unconditional. *(See 1st Corinthians 13:4-7)* The natural man is selfish and will go to the extent of sacrificing others just to preserve himself. He doesn't have it in him to care for anyone but himself.

Dear, you can't afford to marry a man that is not born again and filled with the Spirit of God. A person who is born again is ruled by the Spirit of God and not his fallen human nature. Don't even say "I will change him." That's just self-deception and the consequences are always disastrous. You are not the Holy Spirit and only He can change anyone. The Bible is very clear on this, do not be unequally yoked with an unbeliever *(See 2 Corinthians 6:14).* A man could be very nice but niceness is not a fruit of the Holy Spirit. If he is not born again, it is a dangerous affair. Don't marry him.

Final Word

You might be thinking, "Pastor, it's not that easy to just walk away from someone I really like especially when I already have answers to some of the questions. That should count for something, doesn't it? One does not need to have the answers to all the questions." Each of these questions is very important and knowing the answer to all of them is vital to the success of your relationship. If you are wondering if these kind of men described in this book exist, I can assure you that they do. But it is not your responsibility to go looking for him because it is the man that finds a wife *(See Proverbs 18:22)*. What you can do is to go ahead and live a beautiful life developing your skills and gifts while enjoying a good relationship with God. And as you are busy doing this, that man will find you faster than you can imagine.

I also have a book called *7 Qualities Wise Men Want.* I recommend that you read it after this book because in it you will find the major qualities a wise man looks out for in a woman he wants to marry. And by implication, those are the qualities you should have. It gives you an edge into knowing what you can improve on or what you need to stop doing while you wait for the man of your dreams. Meanwhile, get busy leading the kind of life that gives you fulfilment and brings out the best in you. And as you trust God for the right man for you, I agree with you in line with the Word of God that your expectation will not be cut off.

SURRENDER TO CHRIST

If you read through this book, then you know that a great marriage is a privilege of God's children. The only way to become a child of God is by giving your life to Christ. And if you haven't done that already, the best time to do so is now. You can say this prayer after me:

Lord Jesus, come into my heart. Forgive me my sin. Wash me with your blood. I receive the grace to serve you all the days of my life. Thank you Father, for I am born again in Jesus might name, Amen.

Congratulations! Welcome to the family of God.

Other Books By Kingsley & Mildred Okonkwo

SEVEN QUALITIES WISE MEN WANT

If you find *Seven Qualities Wise Women Ask* interesting and very insightful then you would also find *Seven Qualities Wise Men Want* highly intriguing as it addresses seven undeniable qualities that every wise man looks out for in a potential wife.

Other Books By Kingsley & Mildred Okonkwo

WHO SHOULD I MARRY?

Do you feel like you are literally faced with the option of choosing between the icing and the cake? If you are, then this book is for you. In it, you will discover the Ten Undeniable Qualities that will serve as a guide and "must-have" for your Mr. or Miss Right.

25 WRONG REASONS PEOPLE ENTER RELATIONSHIPS

If you marry for the wrong reasons, you will most likely marry the wrong person. This insightful book will serve as a personal checklist for your motives as it highlights 25 reasons you shouldn't enter a relationship.

Other Books By Kingsley & Mildred Okonkwo

WHEN AM I READY?

- What must I attain, achieve and acquire to be considered ready?
- What are the basic things to look out for in a spouse?

These and more are clearly answered in the book, When Am I Ready? The striking truths in this book will not only make you know if you are ready for marriage, but will also adequately prepare you for it.

Other Books By Kingsley & Mildred Okonkwo

GOD TOLD ME TO MARRY YOU

In Christian circles today, this issue of "GOD SAID" or "GOD TOLD ME" has brought a lot of confusion and caused a lot of problems. The chapters in this book will clear out any doubt from your heart about "GOD SAID" or "GOD TOLD ME".

WAITING FOR ISAAC

Contrary to what many say, God does not save the best for last; He always saves the best for the best times. He may not come when you want Him but He is never late. This book is for every one that has ever asked "What do I do while I wait?"

Other Books By Kingsley & Mildred Okonkwo

SHOULD LADIES PROPOSE?

This is one of the many controversial issues when it comes to relationships and in over a decade of speaking to youths and singles, It has turned out to be a constant question... Do you need answers? Then this book is for you.

Other Books By Kingsley & Mildred Okonkwo

I LOVE YOU BUT MY PARENTS SAY NO

This mini-book helps to answer the pressing question of "How involved should Your parents be in the selection of whom you marry? And practical steps you can take when they object your choice.

Other Books By Kingsley & Mildred Okonkwo

A TO Z OF MARRIAGE

A-Z of marriage is a matter-of-fact and very precise manual, alphabetically arranged for convenience, to help men and women better understand their needs for a better marriage.

Other Books By Kingsley & Mildred Okonkwo

HELP! MY HUSBAND IS ACTING FUNNY

Help! My husband is acting funny is a product of many years of counselling women going through tough times in their marriages. It provides clear, practical and time-tested counsel that has changed the situation of numerous women.

Other Books By Kingsley & Mildred Okonkwo

ALL YEAR ROUND FOR MEN

ALL YEAR ROUND FOR MEN is a 52-WEEK GUIDE ON HOW TO LOVE YOUR WIFE. It is a practical, and easy-to-follow companion for the husband who wants to do right by his wife, making her feel special, loved and protected. It contains 52 tested and trusted tips to help you love your wife all year round.

Other Books By Kingsley & Mildred Okonkwo

MANUAL - THE WAY MEN THINK

A lot of women are stressed in relationships and marriages because they don't understand the way men think. This book addresses the psychology of men and also gives you practical tips you can leverage on.

OTHER BOOKS BY KINGSLEY & MILDRED OKONKWO

- Who Should I Marry?
- When Am I Ready?
- Just Us Girls
- Should Ladies Propose?
- I Love you But My Parents say No
- God Told Me to Marry You
- Waiting For Isaac
- 7 Qualities Wise Men Want.
- 7 Questions Wise Women Ask.
- Chayil - The Virtuous Woman
- Chayil Prayer Journal
- Help! My Husband is Acting Funny
- Hannah's Heart Devotional
- Simply Attractive. (e-book)
- 21 Days Sexual Purity Devotional (e-book)
- All Year Round for Men
- All Year Round for Women
- Manual: The Way Men Think
- 21 Days Prayers and Fasting
- For Expectant Mothers. (e-book)

Printed in Great Britain
by Amazon